HEAR NOW THE Sower

THE RABBI & HIS PARABLE'S INTERPRETATION

MICHEAL PARDUE

Hear Now the Sower
© 2018 by Micheal Pardue
www.michealpardue.com

**Educational
Design & Development**

Published by ED&D Books
www.educationaldd.com

ALL RIGHTS RESERVED. This book contains material protected under International and Federal Copyright Laws and Treaties. Any unauthorized reprint or use of this material is prohibited. No part of this book may be reproduced or transmitted in any form or by any means, electronic or mechanical, including photocopying, recording, or by any information storage and retrieval system without express written permission from the author.

Scripture quotations are from The Holy Bible, English Standard Version® (ESV®), copyright © 2001 by Crossway, a publishing ministry of Good News Publishers. Used by permission. All rights reserved.

Cover design by:

ISBN:0692510079
ISBN-13: 978-0692510070

Printed in the United States of America

To my professors at North Greenville University

Larry S. McDonald
Steve Patton
Keith Lester
Hayne Griffin

Your work and passion instilled in me a strong desire to search out the Scriptures for truth

CONTENTS

The Sower, the Soil, and the Sponge: The Interpretation of the Parable of the Sower in the Context of Rabbinic Literature	1
Comparison Tables	17
Footnotes	24
Mark 4:1-20: A Sermon	37
Bibliography	70

Introduction

Much has been written over the last three centuries in a quest to discover the historical Jesus. Some who have undertaken this quest have come to the conclusion that almost nothing can be known about the historical Jesus of Nazareth. Others have come away from their journey believing that almost everything that is necessary to be known is available to the twenty-first century thinker.[1] Each of these quests provided new insight into the historical world in which Jesus lived. However, many of the scholars who undertook this work ended up remaking Jesus into the image of their theological dispositions.[2]

Most recently, there have been two distinct quests for the historical Jesus. The first arose from the students of Rudolph Bultmann and was shorted lived in the 1950s.[3] The third, and most recent quest, found its rise in the 1980s. This has commonly become known as the third quest.[4] Blomberg writes that this quest is marked by three primary characteristics:

a) a rigorous examination and application of historical criteria to determine the authenticity of the various Gospel data;
b) a reclamation of Jesus the Jew, interpreting him clearly against the backdrop of the

religious ideas and institutions of his day; and

c) a far more nuanced and detailed understand of the diversity of early first-century Judaism.[5]

It is with these distinctives in mind that this paper seeks to compile the work that has been done in one small area of New Testament studies: understanding Jesus' parables in their pedagogical context in connection with the rabbinical teachings of first century Judaism. More specifically, this paper will examine the use by several parable commentators of the *Pirke Avos*[6] in their understanding of Jesus' parable of the Sower.

The Sower

The parables of Christ in the general and the Parable of the Sower in particular have been the source of much study and research since the earliest writings of church history.[7] There are myriads of resources that are available to countless conclusions that are drawn about the nature of the parables and the interpretation of the Parable of the Sower.

In part, the interpretive conclusions that are drawn are derived from the particular conclusion that one draws concerning the authenticity of the interpretation given by Jesus (Mt 13:18-23; Mk

4:13-20; Lk 8:11-15). Many contemporary scholars reject the interpretation given because it frames the parable allegorically.[8] There has, however, been a move by some to accept the biblical text as trustworthy, therefore changing the mindset of parabolic interpretation.[9] The ultimate hermeneutical results of studying the Sower have been varied and far reaching.[10] Those who would allegorize past the interpretation given in the Synoptics have endless access to defining each part of the parable to have meaning. However, if, as Gordon D. Fee and Douglas Stuart write in *How to Read the Bible for All it Worth*, "the believing scholar insists that the biblical texts first of all *mean what they meant*,"[11] then seeking the original interpretation is vitally important.

With the justifiable emphasis to understand Jesus and His teachings within their appropriate historical context, it seems reasonable to study Jesus' parable of the Sower within the context of other relevant teaching during the same period and geographical setting in which Jesus learned and taught. Below is an overview of how the Sower has compared to the rabbinical sayings in *Avos* 5 and how those comparisons have shaped the interpretations put forth by the scholars who explored this connection. First, however, there are a few key resources in understand that Sower that do include rabbinical comparisons to different components of the parable but do not explore the connection to *Avos 5*. Those are explored in the immediately preceding section.

Rabbinical Writing and the Parables

Clearly, if a student of the New Testament desires to have a firm understanding of Jesus' parables and is interested in properly interpreting those parables, he must explore the context in which Jesus lived and taught. Hebrew Scholar David Flusser makes it clear that, "Jewish thought is not—as is often claimed—merely a background for Jesus but is in reality the original context and natural framework of his message."[12] Interestingly, though many of the books written since the dawn of the twentieth century wrestle with the context in which Jesus is teaching the Parable of the Sower, many do not make the connecting point to the fifth chapter of the *Pirkei Avos* which at least at first glance may have relevance for understanding Jesus' words. Obviously, space does not allow to cover every book that has not said something, but the following is an abbreviated overview.

Rabbi Frank Stern's work on the parables[13] is cited throughout the recent literature on parable studies. His chapter on the Parable of the Sower is a treasure trove of background information and rabbinical teaching that has relevance to the parable. His footnotes are rich and informative. However, with all of the connections present in the chapter, he does not mention any connection to the rabbinical teachings of four types prominent in the *Avos.*

Robert Stein's[14] excellent and concise volume on the parables deals with the rabbinic and first-century Jewish culture thoroughly. His walks his readers through a history of parable interpretation, showing the changes that have taken place in the understanding of the parables for each major period in Church history. He provides his readers with a helpful interpretive method: Seek the one main point of the parable, seek to understand the *Sitz im Leben* in which the parable was uttered, seek to understand how the evangelist interpreted the parable, and seek what God is saying to us today through the parable.[15]

David Wenham places his interpretation of the Sower in the context of the coming revolution of the Kingdom.[16] He understands the interpretation given in the Synoptics as fully reflective of Jesus experience in ministry. He gives background information to support this interpretation within the first-century Palestinian context.

Craig Evans writes at length about the parables of early Judaism.[17] He systematically walks the reader though the various types of biblical and postbiblical parables and their features. Also, in the same volume, three chapters deal with the Sower, each using some historical information gleaned from other ancient writings to provide background for the sower.[18]

Kenneth Baily explores the culture of Jesus time period in two separate works on the parables of Luke that have since been combined into a single edition. He writes that:

> To understand the theology of the parables, therefore, we must recapture the culture that informs the text. The culture of the synoptic parables is that of first-century Palestine. Palestinian Christians saw their own culture reflected in the parables and could thereby understand the teller/author's intent directly. But when the cultural base of the Church ceased to be Palestinian the parables inevitably became stories about foreigners.[19]

This problem of the separation between Palestinian Christianity and contemporary Christianity can only be solved by bridging the gap of understanding between the two. Baily uses the bulk of his work in an effort to bridge that gap.

There have also been a number of works that looks specifically at Jesus and His teachings within the rabbinical and cultural context.[20] Though many of these works do not directly address the Sower, they are nonetheless helpful in understanding the culture of the Savior's teachings.

The Case for the Sponge

The advocates for the connection between Jesus' Parable of the Sower and *Avos* build their argument on Jesus' use for four types of soils along with the context of discipleship. Though there six examples given in *Avos* 5,[21] the sixth is most often[22] cited as connecting to Jesus' parable:

> There are four types among students who sit before the sages: A sponge, a funnel, a strainer, and a sieve: a sponge, which absorbs everything; a funnel, which lets in from one end and lets out from the other; a strainer, which lets the wine flow through and retains the sediment; and a sieve, which allows the flower dust to pass through and retains the fine flour.[23]

Recently there have been several advocates for understanding this parable within the context of this specific rabbinical writing.

In the nineteenth century, Anglican archbishop Richard Chenevix Trench connected the Sower parable to *Avos* 5:18 in his work *Notes on the Parables of Our Lord*. The connection is found in a footnote to his writing on the Sower parable: He writes:

> As our Saviour here, so the Jewish doctors divide the hearers of the words of wisdom into four classes. The best they liken to a sponge which drinking in all that it received, again expresses it for others; the worst to a strainer which, letting all the good wine pass through, retains only the ruthless dress; or to a sieve that, passing the fine flour, keeps only the bran.[24]

Interestingly, Trench understands the sponge to be "the best" although this is not the standard understanding presented in the literature.[25] He does not cite specifically those who he has read and referred to as "Jewish doctors." It is unclear if this conclusion has come from the rabbinic texts themselves or from a more recent publication. This would have been most helpful in understanding where his conclusions arise.[26]

Peter Rhea Jones, preaching and New Testament professor at McAfee School of Theology sees a connection between *Avos* 5 and the Sower in *Studying the Parables of Jesus*.[27] Jones writes that while, "the differences in the story are apparent"[28] because of a different setting, the connection is still interesting. For Jones, the connection is significant because "three or the responses are inadequate, and one is exceptional."[29] Jones, like others, only address *Avos* 5.18.

Brad Young is professor of biblical studies in the Graduate School of Theology at Oral Roberts University. A prolific author, he concentrates much of his time to Jewish-Christian interfaith dialogue. Having studied at the Hebrew University, he is intimately familiar with rabbinical studies.

Young explores the rabbinical writing of *Avos* 5.18 in his book, *The Parables*.[30] His chapter on the Parable of the Sower is entitled Four Types of Hears, a reference to the *Avos* which exclaims at the beginning of each of five of the six sayings, "there are four types of …"[31] Young makes it clear that the parable is not primarily about the sower, as the traditional title would imply, but about those who hear. For Young, to understand the Parable of the Sower, "it must be studied in light of Jewish culture."[32] He believes that understanding the

Jewish parallels to this parable make it possible to interpret it properly. He asks:

> Would the people who first heard it have understood the meaning of the parable? A study of Jewish parallels that also use numerous analogies with four types shows that the answer to the question by be affirmative. In a context of Jewish learning and Torah study, four different types of soil conditions would be viewed as various types of disciples absorbing the words taught by their master.[33]

Young then uses this explanation to affirm the interpretation of the parable found in the Synoptic Gospels because it is in line with the explanation given for similar parables in Jewish teachings.[34] Young goes on to demonstrate the parallelism of the parable and demonstrating its relationship to Semitic parallelism. While his argument is convincing, it is not surprising as the Parable of the Sower is being told by a Semitic teacher.

He then turns his attention to *Avos* 5 where he examines three of the six wisdom teachings. He writes:

> Each of the four types of disciple is weighed in the balance in order to determine his positive qualities compared with less desirable characteristics…The strong

> characteristics are weighed against the weaker qualities in four parts. In the world of Jewish learning and Torah scholarship, each person can evaluate his or her strength and weakness…The form and structure of the rabbinic saying is very similar to the four types of soil in the parable of the Sower.[35]

This leads Young then to reject the "ever popular allegorical method"[36] of interpretation. He concludes that:

> [The] method that seeks to discover secret symbolic meanings in the parables actually only conceals the original purpose of Jesus. The parable of the Sower becomes clouded in mystery. People cannot hear its message because the interpreter is forcing his own meaning on each detail of the parable, like *1 Clement*, which imposed a teaching about the future resurrection on the parable. One must listen to Jesus as he tells the parable and see the story in light of rabbinic literature and the rich heritage of the first-century Jesus people. The focus therefore is on Torah learning and discipleship.[37]

Young ties his interpretation directly to the rabbinic literature and his interpretation will be explored at length below under Interpretive Implications.

Coming only slightly after Young's major work on the subject, Klyne Snodgrass, New Testament scholar at North Park Theological Seminary spends extensive time in his significant work *Stories with Intent*[38] on the influence of Jewish thought and writings on the parables of Jesus. Specifically looking at the *Avos*, he finds seven texts that he states are "similar to the similitudes of Jesus."[39] Within this list, he includes *Avos* 5.18. Snodgrass clearly sees this, along with numerous other rabbinical teachings, to be comparable to Jesus parable, however he does not discuss directly why this is so or the effect it has on the Sower's interpretation.

Interpretive and Pastoral Implications

The sower has been interpreted in many different ways throughout the history of the Church.[40] For the purposes of this paper only the interpretive consequences of the relationship of the Sower and *Avos* 5 will be examined below. If a connection is present between one or all of the six sayings in *Avos* 5, does this change how the New Testament student and scholar understands this popular story told by Jesus?

Young gives an extended treatment of the interpretation, rejecting the allegorical interpretation in favor of an interpretation rooted in a rabbinical context. He writes:

> The one message is clear: be like the disciple who receives the word of Jesus' teaching with a good heart. The word sown will produce an abundant return. The word-picture communicates the force of Jesus' teaching in the form of a graphic illustration…[P]arables should be placed in a separate and distinct category. The allegorical approach to the parables pursues the intuitive effort to solve the cryptogram by arbitrarily ascribing meaning to the word-picture. Parables, however, must be studied to hear the message of the storyteller in the context of the situation. Only meaning ascribed by the storyteller by be accepted as showing a correspondence between the picture (mashal) and the reality (*nimshal*). In fact, allegory often misrepresents the original intention of Jesus. If an interpretation is called for, Jesus the master teller of parables gives additional clarity to his example. [41]

Young's interpretation is simple. Jesus is simply telling those who are around him to respond. This is normative part of Jesus ministry.[42]

Jesus "calls upon each person to make a life-changing decision. No one should seek special symbolic meaning for each detail of a parable and allegorize it to suit his or her own purposes."[43]

If Young is to be accepted, the primary emphasis for the parable is the good soil. The question that is left largely unanswered is how he understands the other three types of soil. Based on his interpretation, this question is largely irrelevant because of his primary emphasis.[44]

However, from a homiletical/pastoral standpoint it is difficult to leave the other soils unattended. Young does exemplary work in his treatment of the good soil, even further connecting that them to other rabbinical literature.[45] Others, to the contrary, have went so far as to change the very words that are presented, ignore the context of the message, and jettison the scriptural setting of Jesus' teachings.[46] This makes it imperative from a pastoral perspective to have personal clarity about the composition of the parable and the integrity of the synoptic interpretation. The question becomes, does one have to shake off the more common interpretation of the Sower to accept that there is within the parable a clear connection to the rabbinic teachings present in Jesus day?

A Possible Bridge of Interpretation[47]

It seems as if it is possible to bridge the interpretive processes to allow for a strong connection between the Sower and rabbinical writings while also keeping the traditional homiletical emphasis that examines each of the soils as distinct response to hearing the word of God. This can be done by understanding each of the six sayings from *Avos* 5 as having essentially the same structure. There are two responses that have some merit but are not sufficient, one response that is completely wrong/wicked, and one that is praised in both the rabbinical literature and the Sower parable. This understanding leaves in place the overall theme presented by Young that Jesus calls for a response with a good heart.[48] At the same time, it still takes into account that a great deal of Jesus' parable is devoted to the failure of the sower to see growth along the path and among the rocks and thorns.

It is important to note that the *Avos* sayings do not appear in any particular context with the Mishnah to give the reader an understanding of when and why they were uttered. However, this is not the case with the case with the Sower. In each of the Synoptics there is at least minimal contextualization given.[49]

In *Avos* 5, it is clear that there is nothing to be praised among those types that have insufficient or evil results.⁵⁰ Regardless of one's theological disposition, this is something that New Testament students from both Reformed and Arminian backgrounds can agree. Whether one believes that the rocky and thorny soil people lost their salvation or never had it to begin with, it is obvious that falling away is not an action that is praised by Jesus in His parable.

It seems, therefore, exegetically, historically, and experientially accurate to interpret the Sower parable as following the pattern that is present in *Avos* 5. That is not to claim that Jesus was somehow dependent on the rabbinic teachings that eventually found their way into the Mishnah or vice versa. However, Jesus was a first-century Jew who grew up in constant contact with the religious teachings of His day. Understanding this parable in light of the rabbinic teaching does not change its interpretation but rather it is strengthened.

Conclusion

It can be accepted that there is a relationship between the rabbinical writings and Jesus' parable without ultimately changing the interpretation of the parable itself completely.⁵¹ As has been demonstrated, an interpretation within the context of the rabbinical writings is compatible with an understanding of four responses in the Sower. As in the *Avos* sayings, two responses are inadequate, one is completely wrong, and one is praised. This should give confidence to those whose interpretive goal is to both understand Jesus in His historical/cultural context and properly exegete the text within its scriptural context.

Table 1. *The Sower and the six sayings from Avos 5 broken down by type*

Saying/Parable	1st Type	2nd Type	3rd Type	4th Type
Sower (Mt 13:18-23; Mk 4:13-20; Lk 8:11-15)	Along path	Rocky ground	Among thorns	Good soil
Possessions (Avos 5.13)	Mine and Yours is Mine	Mine is yours and yours is mine	Mine is yours and yours is yours	Yours is mine and mine is mine
Temperament (Avos 5.14)	Angered easy; pacified easily	Hard to anger; hard to pacify	Hard to anger; easy to pacify	Easy to anger; hard to pacify
Student's Understanding (Avos 5.15)	Grasps quickly; forgets quickly	Grasp slowly; forgets slowly	Grasps quickly; forgets slowly	Grasps slowly; forgets quickly

Table 2. *The Sower and the six sayings from Avos 5 broken down by type continued*

Saying/Parable	1st Type	2nd Type	3rd Type	4th Type
Donors to Charity (Avos 5.16)	Wishes to give; wants other no to give	Wishes others to give; does not want to give	Wishes himself to give; wants others to give	Wishes not to give; wants others not to
Attendees of the House of Study (Avos 5.17)	Goes; does not study	Studies; does not go	Goes; studies	Does not go; does not study
Students before the Sages (Avos 5.18)	Sponge	Funnel	Strainer	Sieve

Note: These appear in this table in the same order in which they appear in the text given under saying/parable.

Table 3. *The results of each type from Avos 5.13-15*

Avos		Type	Result
5.13	1	Mine is mine, yours is yours	Average/could be Sodom
	2	Mine is yours, yours is mine	Ignoramus
	3	Mine is yours, yours is yours	Saint
	4	Mine is yours, yours is mine	Sinner
5.14	1	Easy to anger, easy to calm	Neutral
	2	Hard to anger, hard to calm	Neutral
	3	Hard to anger, easy to calm	Saint
	4	Easy to anger, hard to calm	Sinner
5.15	1	Learns quickly, forgets quickly	Neutral
	2	Learns slow, forgets slow	Neutral
	3	Leans quick, forgets slow	Good portion/scholar
	4	Learns slow, forgets quick	Bad portion

Table 4. *The results of each type from Avos 5.16-18 continued*

Avos		Type	Result
5.16	1	Gives, no one else should give	Begrudges others
	2	Others give, but not him	Begrudges himself
	3	Gives, others give	Saint
	4	Does not give, others do not give	Sinner
5.17	1	Goes but does not study	Reward only for going
	2	Studies, but does not go	Reward only for studying
	3	Goes and studies	Saint
	4	Does not go and does not study	Sinner
5.18	1	Sponge	Soaks up all
	2	Funnel	Pours out all
	3	Strainer	Keeps the bad
	4	Sieve	Keeps the good

Note: In the first five, the type in position one and two are somehow incomplete. The type in position three is described in the best terms. Position four is a sinner or a bad portion.

Table 5. *The Sower parable with explanations of type from Luke 8*

Type	Explanation[1]	Explanation of the Type[2]	Result
Along path	Seed is trampled underfoot, the birds devoured it.	The devil comes and takes away the word from their hearts, so that they may not believe and be saved.	Do not grow
Rocky ground	As it grew up it withered away because it had no moisture.	They receive the word with joy. However, they have no root. They believe for a while but fall away during a time of testing.	Fall away

---

[1] Adapted from Luke 8:5-8.

[2] Adapted from Luke 8:12-15.

Table 6. *The Sower parable with explanations of type from Luke 8*

Type	Explanation[3]	Explanation of the Type[4]	Result
Among thorns	The thorns grow up and choke out the seed.	These are choked by the cares and riches and pleasures of like and their fruit does not mature.	Do not mature
Good soil	Grows up and yields a hundredfold.	Hear the word and hot it fast in an honest and good heart. They bear fruit with patience.	Bear fruit

---

[3] Adapted from Luke 8:5-8.
[4] Adapted from Luke 8:12-15.

Table 7. *The sixth Avos saying arranged in the order given in the Talmud with explanation*

Type	Explanation	Explanation of the Type	Result
Sponge	Absorbs all	The student absorbs all that he studies	None given
Sieve	Passes through the fine flour are retains the coarse particles	An intelligent student retains what is good in the study and leaves out what is not	Intelligent
Funnel	Lets in the liquid through one opening and lets it out through the other	The unintelligent student. What enters his one ear goes out through the other, until all is gone.	Unintelligent
(Wine) Strainer	Lets the wine pass through and absorbs the dregs	The wicked student forgets the good teachings and retains the bad ones	Wicked

Note: The explanations given in the Talmud bring the understanding of this sixth saying closer into the format of the previous five. Though the order still does not follow the same as the previous sayings, they are now grouped closer to the results presented in Table 3. With the given explanations it would be appropriate to number the results of this saying as: Sponge-1; Funnel-2; Sieve-3; and Strainer-4.

---

[1] Craig Blombery, *Jesus and the Gospels* (Nashville, TN: Broadman & Holman, 2009), 205.

[2] Albert Schweitzer, *The Quest of the Historical Jesus* (Mineola, NY: Dover Publications).

[3] Blomberg, *Jesus and the Gospels*, 209-10

[4] Blomberg provides a thorough, though no exhaustive survey of the works that have been written about the "Third Quest." These include: B. Witherington III, *The Jesus Quest: The Third Search for the Jew of Nazareth*, rev. ed. (Downers Grove: IVP, 1997); D.B. Gowler, *What Are They Saying about the Historical Jesus?* (New York: Paulist, 2007); and M.J. McClymond, *Familiar Stranger: An Introduction to Jesus of Nazareth* (Grand Rapids and Cambridge: Eerdmans, 2004).

[5] Ibid., 210.

6. Throughout the literature involving the *Pirkei Avos*, different numbering is used depending on which translation the author is referring to. The work itself is often referred to as the *Pirkei Avot*, the *Pirkei Avoth* or the *Pirkei Avos*. In English the work may appear as *Ethics of the Fathers* or *Chapters of the Fathers*. This paper will consistently use *Pirkei Avos* or simply *Avos*. The reader should be aware that the title and/or number may be different in other translations and in the sources referenced in the paper.

7. Young writes that I Clement had commented on the Parable of the Sower in speaking about the Resurrection (Brad H. Young, *The Parables: Jewish Tradition and Christian Interpretation* (Grand Rapids: Baker, 1998). Irenaeus wrote concerning the interpretation of parables in *Against Heresies* (Alexander Roberts & W.H. Rambaut, *Translations of the Writings of the Fathers: Down to A.D. 325.ed.* Roberts, Alexander and James Donaldson (Edinburgh: T&T Clark) 1884.) Though not a commentary, the Parable of the Sower is largely preserved in the *Gospel of Thomas*. However, Young points out that Thomas' version "betrays clear evidence of editorial modification." (Young, *Parables*, 255.)

[8] Snodgrass points out that, "Since Jülicher's work a good deal of NT scholarship has rejected the interpretation as early church allegorizing" (Snodgrass, *Parables*, 164). He goes on to examine the chief complaints against the interpretation provided in the Synoptics and concludes, "The interpretation fits the parable and has every claim to be in some form the explanation Jesus gave his disciples (166).

[9] Luz writes, "Along with others I assume that the fourfold parable of the seed was meant exactly as it was interpreted in Mark 4:13-20. From the beginning it was a 'parable about parables,' or a *meditation about the various hearers of Jesus' proclamation.* The interpretation fits the original character of the fourfold parable exactly" (Luz. *Matthew 8-20*. 244. italics his). See also: Philip B. Payne, "The Authenticity of the Parable of the Sower and Its Interpretation," in *Gospel Perspectives*, vol. 1, ed. R.T. France and David Wenham (Sheffield: JSOT, 1980), 163-207.

[10] For an interesting treatment of the Mormon interpretation of the Sower, see Jared M. Halverson, "Of Soils and Souls: The Parable of the Sower," *The Religious Educator* 9, no. 3 (2008): 31-47, accessed March 19, 2015, https://ojs.lib.byu.edu/spc/index.php/RelEd/article/viewFile/2258/2133. Alyce M. McKenzie, who has written several books on the parables and wisdom literature advocates for rebranding the parable of the Sower: http://www.patheos.com/Resources/Additional-Resources/Rebranding-the-Parable-of-the-Sower-Alyce-McKenzie-07-04-2011

[11] Gordon D. Fee and Douglas Stuart, *How to Read the Bible for All Its Worth* (Grand Rapids: Zonderzan, 2014), 14.

[12] Flusser, David in Young, *The Parables,* ix.

[13] Frank Stern, *A Rabbi Looks at Jesus' Parable* (Oxford: Rowman & Littlefield, 2006).

[14] Robert H. Stein, *An Introduction to the Parables of Jesus* (Philadelphia: Westminster Press, 1981)

[15] Ibid., 72-81

[16] David Wenham, *The Parables of Jesus* (Downers Grove: IVP Academic, 1989), 41-48.

[17] Craig Evans, "Parables in Early Judaism," in *The Challenges of Jesus' Parables*, ed. Richard N. Longenecker (Grand Rapids: William B Eerdmans Publishing Company, 2000), 51-78.

[18] To show the varied opinions on the understanding of the interpretation provided in the Synoptics, Hooker considers the interpretation a later addition (93); Hagner sees the interpretation as authentic to Jesus, writing that the parable, "makes quite good sense in the mouth of Jesus...It is simply unjustifiable prejudice to conclude that Jesus never allegorized a parable" (105); and Longenecker does not state a position explicitly.

[19] Kenneth E. Baily, *Poet & Peasant and Through Peasant Eyes: A Literary-Cultural Approach to the Parables in Luke* (Grand Rapids: William B Eerdmans Publishing Company, 1983), 27.

[20] A multitude of other works explore Jesus' teachings in the context of rabbinical teachings and Jesus' historical context. cf. David Flusser, *The Sage of Galilee: Rediscovering Jesus' Genius* (Grand Rapids: William B. Eerdmans Publishing Company, 2007).; Brad H. Young, *Meet the Rabbis: Rabbinic Thought and the Teachings of Jesus* (Grand Rapids: Baker Academic, 2007).; Brad H. Young, *Jesus the Jewish Theologian* (Grand Rapids: Baker Academic, 1995).; Bruce Chilton, *Rabbi Jesus An Intimate Biography: The Jewish Life and Teachings that Inspired Christianity* (New York: Doubleday, 2000).; David Zaslow, *Jesus: First Century Rabbi* (Brewster: Paraclete Press, 2014).

[21] *Pirkei Avos* 5.13-18.

[22] Young gives a thorough overview of the four types theme that is present throughout the rabbinical writings. He, more than most, digs deeply into this prevalent theme, assisting his readers in seeing how "the four types weigh against each other like the different sides of a balance scale" (265). (Young, *The Parables,* 265-68).

[23] *Prikei Avos* 5.18.

[24] Richard Chenevix Trench, *Notes on the Parables of Our Lord* (New York: D. Appleton and Company, 1878), 84.

[25] The Talmud gives an expanded explanation of the four types of character among students: "One resembles a sponge: as a sponge absorbs all liquids, so does that kind of student absorb all that he studies: Scripture, Mishnah, Midrash, Halakhoth, and Agadoth. One is like a sieve: as a sieve passes through the fine flour and retains the coarse particles, so an intelligent student retains what is good in the study and leaves out what is not. One is like a funnel: as it lets in the liquid through one opening and lets it out through the other, so is it with the unintelligent student--what enters his one ear goes out through the other, until all is gone. The fourth student is like a wine-strainer which lets the wine pass through and absorbs the dregs: so also the wicked student forgets the good teachings and retains the bad ones." This presents a judgment on three of the four types of students (sieve—intelligent; funnel—unintelligent; and wine-strainer—wicked) while not giving a judgment on the student who is like the sponge.

[26] Trench's order does follow that of the Avos and the interpretation given in the Talmud by putting the sponge first. However, the Talmud's interpretation is positive toward the sieve and then negative toward the funnel and wine-strainer.

[27] Peter Rhea Jones. *Studying the Parables of Jesus* (Macon: Smyth & Helwys, 1999) is a major revision of his work *Teaching the Parables of Jesus* (Nashville: Broadman Press, 1982). The original did not contain a discussion of *Avos* 5 and the relationship with the Sower.

[28] Jones, *Studying the Parables*, 68.

[29] Ibid.

[30] Young, *The Parables.*

[31] *Pirkei Avos* 5.14-18.

[32] Young, *The Parables,* 253.

[33] Ibid., 251.

[34] Ibid., 252.

[35] Ibid., 265-66.

[36] Ibid., 268. He argues that the interpretation given by Jesus is in fact not allegorical. He writes, "The parables of Jesus, like their counterparts in rabbinic literature are unique. Some teaching forms, such as fables or allegories, are somewhat similar to Gospel and rabbinic parables, but not the classic form of story parables, such as those in the Gospels and rabbinic literature, is a distinct type of teaching technique that has no parallel (271)."

[37] Ibid.

[38] Snodgrass, Klyne. *Stories with Intent: A Comprehensive Guide to the Parables of Jesus* (Grand Rapids: Eerdmans, 2008).

[39] Ibid., 56.

[40] The number of interpretations is too numerous to exhaustively discuss here. However, because, "the Sower is a parable for all parables, a parable about parables and a parabling" (John Dominic Crossan, *The Power of Parable: How Fiction by Jesus Became Fiction about Jesus*. New York: HarperOne, 2012, 20) it is vital to considering the broader implications of the interpretive method utilized.

[41] Young, *The Parables, 271.*

[42] Mt. 4:19-22, 9:9; Mk 1:16-20

[43] Young, *The Parables*, 275.

[44] cf. Snodgrass, *Stories,* 169. He argues that, "any valid interpretation must do justice—not merely to the harvest—but to the emphasis given the threefold failure, failure that occurs at increasingly later stages in the growth process...To determine what Jesus' original hearers would have understood is impossible because we do not know what other comments were made or information was given in connection with the parable" (169).

[45] Ibid., 274-75.

[46] Donald H. Juel, "Encountering the Sower: Mark 4:1-20," *Interpretation* 56, no. 3 (July 2002): 273-283. has writing a wonderful article on the issues, both scholarly and pastoral with removing the parable from its scriptural context.

[47] cf. Tables 3 and 4 in particular to see the connection.

[48] Young, *The Parables*, 274-75.

⁴⁹ In Matthew: That same day Jesus went out of the house and sat beside the sea. 2 And great crowds gathered about him, so that he got into a boat and sat down. And the whole crowd stood on the beach. And he told them many things in parables (13:1-3a); in Mark: Again he began to teach beside the sea. And a very large crowd gathered about him, so that he got into a boat and sat in it on the sea, and the whole crowd was beside the sea on the land. And he was teaching them many things in parables, and in his teaching he said to them (4:1-2); and in Luke: And when a great crowd was gathering and people from town after town came to him, he said in a parable (8:4). Obviously, there is an even larger context that each pericope is located.

⁵⁰ The sponge, which soaks up everything, may come closest, but the Talmud is silent at this point.

⁵¹ Jones' point in presenting the *Avos* text is to show that one response is "exceptional" while the other three are "inadequate" (Jones, *Studying the Parables*, 68). He comes to the conclusion that the along-the-path people where those who had not yet believed and been saved. Contra. Young, *Parables* above.

Micheal Pardue

Mark 4:1-20

This second section of Hear Now the Sower is the sermon I preached from Mark 4:1-20. I hope this gives some insight on my understanding of the text after considering the possible roots of rabbinic literature. Though the sermon is edited for readability, I have made every attempt to capture the spoken-word nature of the sermon. I do not preach from a manuscript, so it is necessary to polish after the preaching event. If you would like to listen to the original sermon, it is available at www.michealpardue.com

As we come to Mark, Chapter 4, we read where Jesus gave one of the largest sections of teaching in the Gospel of Mark. Teaching is an important emphasis for Mark's Gospel and the ministry of Jesus overall. As we have journeyed together in Mark's Gospel, we have seen that Jesus has teach before, but it has primarily been in the context of the narrative that Mark is telling us. So as Mark has been walking us through his gospel, he has been telling us these stories about what Jesus did when he healed people and cast out demons. There has been some teaching referred to in those situations, but for the most part we have not had a lot of that teaching. That changes when we get to Mark chapter 4 beginning in verse 1, so I invite you this morning if you would and are able to stand with me in reverence to God's Word as we begin reading in verse 1.

¹Again he began to teach beside the sea. And a very large crowd gathered about him, so that he got into a boat and sat in it on the sea, and the whole crowd was beside the sea on the land. ²And he was teaching them many things in parables, and in his teaching he said to them: ³"Listen! Behold, a sower went out to sow. ⁴And as he sowed, some seed fell along the path, and the birds came and devoured it. ⁵Other seed fell on rocky ground, where it did not have much soil, and immediately it sprang up, since it had no depth of soil. ⁶And when the sun rose, it was scorched, and since it had no root, it withered away. ⁷Other seed fell among thorns, and the thorns grew up and choked it, and it yielded no grain. ⁸And other seeds fell into good soil and produced grain, growing up and increasing and yielding thirtyfold and sixtyfold and a hundredfold." ⁹And he said, "He who has ears to hear, let him hear."

¹⁰And when he was alone, those around him with the twelve asked him about the parables. ¹¹And he said to them, "To you has been given the secret of the kingdom of God, but for those outside everything is in parables, ¹²so that

> *"they may indeed see but not perceive,*
> *and may indeed hear but not understand,*
> *lest they should turn and be forgiven."*

¹³And he said to them, "Do you not understand this parable? How then will you understand all the parables? ¹⁴The sower sows the word. ¹⁵And these are the ones along the path, where the word is sown: when they hear, Satan immediately comes and takes away the word that is sown in them. ¹⁶And these are the ones sown on rocky ground: the ones who, when they hear the word, immediately receive it with joy. ¹⁷And they have no root in themselves, but endure for a while; then, when tribulation or persecution arises on account of the word, immediately they fall away. ¹⁸And others are the ones sown among thorns. They are those who hear the word, ¹⁹but the cares of the world and the deceitfulness of riches and the desires for other things enter in and choke the word, and it proves unfruitful. ²⁰But those that were sown on the good soil are the ones who hear the word and accept it and bear fruit, thirtyfold and sixtyfold and a hundredfold."

Very often when Jesus spoke, He utilized a literary form known as a parable. This is the first main parable that we have come to in Mark's gospel and it is one that, if you have been in church for very much of your life, you have heard before. We often refer to it, and you may see it referred to in your Bible as The Parable of the Sower. As we dig into this parable and we consider Jesus' teaching it may be more appropriate to understand it as The Parable of the Soils. Actually, the sower gets very little attention. For us this morning, the sower is one that probably most of us should pay good attention to. This parable tells us a lot about our job—our responsibility—as believers in Christ.

I think it is very fitting that we would come to this parable on the day our mission team is sharing about our upcoming trip to El Salvador where we will be frequently preaching the gospel. This parable serves as a reminder of our responsibility to be faithful in sharing the Gospel and leave the results to Christ's movement in the heart of those who hear.

Look, with me as we begin in verse one. We have this an introduction provided by Mark. Jesus begins to teach beside the sea. There is this large crowd that has gathered around Him. The crowd is so large that Jesus is forced to back up from the seashore. He is forced to get into a boat and float out on the water and there He sits down and begins to teach them.

Think about what it would have took for Jesus to have talked to this very large crowd while He is out on the water. Now most likely the place that He is teaching is kind of naturally made for that type of thing. The terrain is such that people can stand there on the seashore, maybe on the hill beside the sea, and listen to Jesus teach. Remember there is no microphone, no "PA" system. Everyone is sitting quietly and being very attentive.

So, Jesus is in the boat and He sits down, and He begins to teach to them. But we know He taught more than this. There is apparently more included after the teaching that takes place in our text.

He tells them first this parable that we refer to as the sower. The Bible says in verse two that, **He was teaching them many things in parables, and in His teaching He said to them:** So a part of it there is a lot more going on but this is the central focus that Mark gives us that His teaching was on this particular parable.

He begins this particular parable by saying very firmly, **listen!** He is calling their attention so that they would be completely focused on what He is saying. You and I should do that sort of thing when the Word of God is speaking to us. We need to tune out other things and listen to this. Jesus wants them to know that what He is about to say is going to be very important. As a matter of fact, in verse nine when He finishes telling the parable He comes back to that first notion again when He says, **And He said to them, "He who has ears to hear, let him hear.**

Now if you are doing your read-through-the-Bible-in-a-year, you may read that one word—listen—and just keep reading. However, this is where your ears should perk up. This is where you, if you have been reading for a while, need to adjust your vision and adjust your mind and come back to what you are doing instead of just reading through the words. Jesus is about to say something important. I believe that this parable of the sower is fundamentally important for our understanding of evangelism and human nature.

As I began to read this parable, read about its context, read how others had dealt with it throughout history, and fought through this parable, it encouraged me. It shows us the sovereignty of God. So, we will look at the parable itself and then we are going to look at the explanation that Jesus gives.

So, what happens? Four things happen. There is this guy, he is known to us as the sower and he goes out into his field and he begins to scatter seed. That does not seem to be that impressive, right? That is pretty common. But he is just throwing it out. You get the impression that Jesus' sower is just scattering it everywhere. There were some in Jesus' day who carried out the practice Jesus is talking about. They would actually scatter their seed and then go back and plow over the field so that everything would be buried. It did not happen like this all the time but that may be what Jesus is talking about in His parable.

So, the guy is out in his field and he is just throwing the seed out of his bag, scattering it out everywhere. When you do that, you are not going to have nice neat rows, you are not going have everything real orderly. There is going be some of your seed that works and some of it that does not, right? You do not have to have lived in the society that Jesus lived in to understand that is what is going to happen, right?

If you are just throwing it out everywhere some of it is going to land on the road and some of it is going to land over in the bushes. It is going to land anywhere and everywhere and that is what happens in this parable.

Along the Path

So, some of the seed falls alongside the road or alongside the path. It is really easy to spot, it is just lying there unobscured. We are told that the birds come. This is verse four, the birds came and devoured it. That is what happens when you just throw it out. Sometimes it is not going to do anything. Someone or something is going to come by and get it or it is going to land on a hard road, or it is going to land somewhere, and it does not get buried and the seeds do not take.

Rocky Ground

Next, in verse five, other seed fell on rocky ground. This ground is hard. We get the picture that there is a thin layer of dirt and under it is rocky, hard ground. You need it to get buried deeper so that it has a good place for roots to take hold, but that does not happen here. It is very shallow soil. He says that it immediately sprang up. It comes up very quickly and but it had no root. When the sun comes up, as we see in verse six, it withers away.

The Weeds

Other seed, goes over in the bushes—over in the weeds. It starts to grow up but it is choked out. If you drove by my garden this summer, this was my garden at the end of the summer. The weeds took over and you had to pick through the weeds to try to find anything, if there was even anything there. This is what happens when the seeds are among the weeds.

The Good Soil

Now last seed, some of it, - cause the guy is not incompetent right, he's not an incompetent farmer, he's not the worst farmer ever – so some of it falls on good soil and it says it sprouts up. Verse eight: **and other grain fell in the good soil and produced grain, or other seed fell and produced grain growing up and increasing and yielding thirtyfold and sixtyfold and a hundredfold.** So thirtyfold is pretty good. Sixtyfold was really good. And a hundredfold basically would have made his audience perk their ears up–wow! Not only was this guy pretty good but we want to get our farming advice from him.

Somehow, he threw this stuff over in the road, he threw some of this stuff over in the bushes, he threw some of it where there is a bunch of rocks, and he still saw a hundredfold production.

Interlude

So that all sounds really nice right? You and I hear that story and–okay–Jesus told them a nice story. We might not, however, understand what it means. We are fortunate with this parable that Jesus gives us the meaning of the parable. We will get to that in a moment but before He does, before He gives us the meaning, we have a little interlude here that begins in verse ten.

His disciples hear this and they walk away from it like you and I might. If we just had the parable and we had no instrument for interpreting it, we may not come away from it with a proper meaning. So His disciples are confused and they come to Him in verse ten and they ask Him about the parables. He says in verse eleven, **To you has been given the secret of the kingdom of God, but for those outside everything is in parables.** This is where we run into one of the most difficult portions of all of the Gospel of Mark to under. We are about to read a passage here, you see it in your Bible in the next two verses, from Isaiah chapter six. If you know anything about Isaiah chapter six, (you may not realize that you do but it is one of probably the most we known passages in Isaiah) Isaiah goes into the temple and he sees God. He is mesmerized by what he sees.

We have this picture of the train of God's robe filling up the temple and God's presence filling up the temple and there are angels flying around and Isaiah is dumbstruck by what he is witnessing in front of him. And when he gets to the end of this vision, God asks for someone to go and to preach to the people. And Isaiah says, **God, here am I send me.** In Isaiah chapter six you see that what God tells him to do is to go preach to people that are not going to listen. Now that sounds ridiculous does it not? He tells Isaiah, I want you to go preach to people who are not going to listen to you. Now there is plenty of preachers who may say "I do that every Sunday, it is not a big deal." But Isaiah is given a grave message and he is told to go preach it even though no one is going to listen. What an utterly sad commission.

Jesus quotes that passage here, when He says to you who are a part of God's family, you who are a part of the kingdom you have understanding but to everyone else I am speaking in parables. But why? He answers this in verse twelve, **So that they may indeed see but not perceive, and may indeed hear but not understand lest they should turn and be forgiven.**

For two thousand years this verse has caused trouble to people in the church. Why? What is it saying? It sounds as if this verse is saying that Jesus is speaking in parables so that some people will not understand Him and turn to Him. For two thousand years people have tried to soften the blow of this passage. Because frankly that does not sound like the Jesus we think we know. It does not sound like something Jesus would say or Jesus would do. Yet He is quoting Isaiah where God says that very thing to Isaiah.

The parable of the sower is much easier than some of the others that you will encounter in the Gospels. He is telling His disciples very clearly that unless people have faith—unless they believe—when they hear these parables, when they hear Him teaching about the kingdom of God, it will be as foolishness to them. And they often were thought of that way. Read the parables throughout all the gospels. You see these religious leaders as they hear Jesus' teaching and they do not understand. They do not want to understand. They reject it. They push it away. And Jesus is saying to those people there is going to be no understanding. They are just not going to understand the things of God.

However, to the disciples—to those who are following after Jesus—He says this in verse thirteen, **Do you not understand this parable?** That had to hurt a little bit, right? **Do you not understand this parable? How then will you understand all parables?**

Before we go through these four explanations, this should be a caution to us. When we come upon parts of God's Word that we do not understand we should challenge ourselves to understand. If you do not think they exist either you are a lot smarter than I am or you just have not read far enough to find the hard parts. There are many parts of God's Word that are hard to understand. These parts should challenge us and push us on. It should break our heats if we ever get comfortable in not understanding something God has said. We should not be comfortable not understanding something that God has said. I am not promising that we are going to figure it out. I am not saying we are going to get all the answers. However, if we just become comfortable, never thinking and exploring what God has said in His Word we should be upset by that.

I have been teaching through Genesis on Sunday nights and we have come to plenty of places where I just do not understand it. I am just not sure if it can be understood completely. That does not mean that I want to have a place in my life where I am still not curious and interested in understanding what God has said.

Jesus challenges them here. How do you not understand this parable? You have been walking with me. You have been following after me. I have been teaching these things. How do you not understand this? We should be challenged by that. I have met far too many people in my time working in churches that were simply satisfied being ignorant about things that God has said. Those people have a cheap and shallow faith. We should want to know more and more and more about what God has said and who He is. We should want to know more about the One who has made us in His image. The Creator who has sent His Son to die for us. Let it not be said of us what Jesus is saying to His disciples: **How do you not understand?** Let it not be from a lack of trying.

Who Am I?

In His compassion He gives them the interpretation of the parable. He does not do that for every parable. We are fortunate in the fact that He takes the time with His disciples to walk through what He means in this parable. It is paramount that we understand the explanation that He gives in verses fourteen through twenty because this explanation helps us to understand our role in this parable and our understanding of all parables.

For me, the question I have before the interpretation is, where do I fall? Where am I at in this parable? So before we go into the four soils I want to tell you where you are at in this parable. If you know Christ, you are like the sower. You might say, "I thought Jesus was the sower." You are right. Jesus is the sower, and so are you. You say well I know I've cheated pastor, I went to the end and I read verse twenty and I am the good soil. I can accept that, but I want you to walk away from the message this morning understanding that you are also the sower.

The Interpretation – Path People

First, verse fourteen, the sower sows the Word. The sower is the guy out there in the field with his bag of seeds and he is just throwing it out. There is some urgency here with this sower. He is not going through and putting one little bit here and then going to the next place. There is this urgency as he spreads this seed out anywhere he can get it.

It happens to fall one of four places. The first place that the seed, which we have been told by Jesus is the Word is on the along-the-path people. You see that in verse fifteen. The along-the-path people are obviously the ones along the path where the Word is sown. **When they hear, Satan immediately comes and takes away the word that is sown in them.** These people simply do not respond. The spreading of the Word in their life—the seeding of the Word into their soil—has no effect on these people. They reject it. Jesus says that Satan comes and he takes it away from them. They refuse. They refuse to believe. It simply has no effect on them that the Word has been sown in their life.

They could be sitting in a service like this and they could hear God's Word preached to them and it will just simply have no effect. They simply do not care. It never even penetrated their heart. It is a strange thing to think. However, if you have been in ministry very long or been a Christian very long, you have encountered many of these people. You can put God's Word in front of them and they just they reject it every time. Every time it is there, Satan just takes it away.

It is a pretty drastic statement by Jesus. It is hard for me to think about the fact that there are people out there who simply do not want to hear God's Word. We must not limit this to people in foreign countries from other religions. There are people here who you have witnessed to and there are people I have witnessed to that continually reject God's Word.

Now we need to be careful here in our understanding. We do not know where people ultimately fall in Jesus' interpretation. We do not know what God is going to do in someone's heart. It may be that it is just taking them a long time to receive God's Word. Our experience tells us there are people who just do not want any part of it. This is obviously a wrong response to the Word but these along the path people they exist and their reaction is heart wrenching.

The Interpretation – Rocky People

The people we find in verses sixteen and seventeen are the rocky ground people. Quite frankly, this is where the people become more confusing. Look what He says in verse sixteen. **And these are the ones sown on rocky ground: the ones who, when they hear the word, immediately receive it with joy.** That sounds good, right? If we stop in verse sixteen and we do not read on or look at the context, it all sounds good. They hear the Word of God and they immediately receive it with joy. Perfect. That is exactly what we want. That is what we want people to do. We want people to hear the Word and we want them to receive it with joy.

But it does not stop. Look in verse seventeen. **And they have no root in themselves, but endure for a while; then, when tribulation or persecution arises on account of the word, immediately they fall away.** These people receive God's Word with joy. They seem to have some life in them. There seems to be something taking place. They receive God's Word with joy but their roots do not go very deep. They endure for a while but when hardship comes they stumble.

I do not know how long you have been in church. Maybe this is your first time ever stepping foot in the church if so, this mindset may seem odd. But for me, thirty-one years of church participation, this sounds really familiar. Think about the number of people who come to a revival service, or who come down on a Sunday morning to be saved. They are just full of emotion and they are crying and they are have this powerful emotional experience. However, three months, six months, a year down the road, you cannot find them.

They have this "reception" of the Word and they do so with joy but they never grow very deep. Their roots never grow very deep and they do not last very long. Everything for them was built on that emotional response and quite frankly an emotional response to the Gospel is not a saving response to the gospel. It is a heart response that causes us to be saved. It is receiving the grace and forgiveness that God has given us. It is turning from our sin and believing in Christ. It is not crying or feeling good inside. I am not saying those things do not happen.

I remember one time I was speaking at a camp and I had given an invitation and it was not exactly the invitation that the camp director wanted me to give because I was not really looking for emotion. He ended up doing the "emotional response" later in the week and that did not work out real well. I was looking for a response to the

Gospel. At the end of my message, this young man came forward. He was ten or twelve years old and we began to talk. I ask, "Why did you come forward?"

He said, "I want to be saved."

So I asked, "What does that mean?"

He began to explain to *me* the Gospel. I told this kid, "I am not going to lead you in a prayer. I want you to pray." Guess what he prayed! He prayed the Gospel and it was so wonderful. Guess who was crying? Me. I was bawling.

This young man understood what Christ had done for him. He knew that he, even at his young age, he understood enough to ask Christ to forgive him without me giving him some special formula.

Later in the week we did it the other way. All these children came forward. It was just amazing. I mean it would have been like everyone in this room came forward to be saved. As we began to talk to these young children this time, some six and seven, eight, we asked, "Why did you come forward tonight?"

The first little boy told me, "Well because my friend walked to the front."

So I went on, "What are you wanting to do?"

"Well I want to be saved."

"What does that mean?" I asked.

"Well I do not know," he replied.

And I remember sitting with the counselor from that church afterwards and he said, "Pastor, I do not know if any of these boys were saved. I do not think I can take them back and baptize them in our church. I just do not think that is fair to them."

I said, "I think you are right. I am excited that they have this desire to know more about Christ and to learn more about Him and to begin following Him in their young lives, but I do not know if what they have done is what we would call saving faith. I do not know if they have repented and believed the Gospel."

Now if you lined all of those children up today and I had to take the money in my bank account and put on which one had entered into the Kingdom of God that week, I would put it on the boy who had begun with roots planted deep. Maybe all of those boys were saved that night. I pray that that is the case. I would put my confidence on the one who had begun with roots plant deep.

Friends, we have too many rocky soil people. We need to ensure that we do not contribute to someone being in the rocky soil. We oftentimes have the opportunity to push the seed deeper so that the roots are planted better but we do not. Jesus says that these people, when it comes to the tribulation that caused by following after Christ, the fall away. How many of them, the first time their faith is challenged in the public arena they have no idea how to defend it? How many times do they fall away are confronted with the secularism that is prevalent in our society, they are confronted with that, it pushes back against their faith and they have no defense—no deep roots? How many times does that happen? Way too often.

Now, do not misunderstand, I believe we are responsible for so much of this by not planting seeds deeper but the Bible is clear and puts all the responsibility on the soil. I am saying we have got to do a better job discipling. We have got to do a better job of teaching our kids and young Christians. But the Bible puts the emphasis on the soil. They grow up for a little while and then they fade away. When things get tough. When tribulations get tough they cannot face it and they fade away.

The Interpretation – Thorny People

Now we have the thorny ground people. Verses eighteen and nineteen, **And others are the ones sown among thorns. They are those who hear the word, but the cares of the world and**

the deceitfulness of riches and the desires for other things enter in and choke the word, and it proves unfruitful. They hear the Word. They hear it preached. They hear it taught. Maybe they hear it once or they hear it a lot. They hear it but everything else in the world gets in the way. To me, these things are getting progressively worse. The first people just reject it; Satan steals it from them. The second group they begin to grow but they cannot handle the persecution. These people they hear it but it is just not as good as other things.

They hear the good news of the Gospel but the good news of the gospel is just not as important as their money. The good news of the Gospel is just not as important as their favorite recreational activity. The Gospel is good and it sounds good but it is just not as good as a number of other things in their life.

Jesus lays out some of the specifics:
But the cares of this world cause you to fall away. The excuses follow like this, "I have other things to do. The Gospel may be good but I have other stuff that is just simply more important. I have a hard life, do not you know that, God? I like your Word and everything. It is nice, but the cares of this world are so much more important."

The deceitfulness of riches cause you to fall away. The excuses follow like this, "God, I would rather become wealthy than allow your Word to be sown in my heart. God, I can do so much with my wealth." I think one of the things we have to be careful with as Christians is assuming that we can substitute wealth, even giving it away, for obedience to God.

"Well, God, I give a lot to your work." While all the time God's demanding obedience. He tells that to His children, correct? When Israel, they are giving sacrifices and they are doing such a great job with that, and He says, no, I'd rather have obedience. He says the deceitfulness of wealth, the deceitfulness of riches chokes it out.

The desires for other things enter in cause you to fall away. If you follow after God there are going to be some things that you are going to want to do and He is going to say, "no!" You are going to say, "Well, I want to do this, or I want to do that, I want to have this relationship, or I want to do this destructive activity."

However, God is going to say, "No, I am more important! I am the One in charge. I am the One who made you. I am the One who demands your obedience. Not that thing or person or activity."

Jesus says for those who are the thorny ground people, those weeds of deceit, of destruction, and of any other thing grow right up. Think about the number of people who are sitting at home instead of being in church as a direct act of disobedience toward God. Look at the book of Hebrews, not fellowshipping with other believers is disobedience to God. Think about how many people are sitting at home today who refuse to fellowship and worship with other believers because they have allowed some little weed to grow up and become more important. They have the security of the powerful oak that is the Gospel and they worry about a little insignificant weed. They have allowed this little worthless thing to choke it out.

I think about the garden at my house. By the end of the summer the weeds had overtaken the garden and we would occasionally walk through and just to see if anything made it. Did anything survive? It looked like Armageddon in my garden. We would just pick up the pieces to see if anything survived the explosion. Every now and then we would find something in there. We would be digging around discover that something that made it.

That is how a lot of people treat the Christian faith. They think you can walk up to someone's life even though you can see that this garden is covered by weeds—nasty and horrible—you can find something. Seemingly, nothing good is in there at all. It completely covered. However, they will wade in their knee high weeds and reach down and find this little vegetable that has survived and try to use that. "Hey look! Look see I have got it all together. See, look, I am practicing my Christian."

It does not matter the weeds have overtaken. It does not matter there is nothing edible at all. They will find some little thing that survived and say, "Hey this is my Christian faith. Look it made it through the weeds. Look, I can still have all of these weeds that are choking out everything and still have my relationship with Christ. Look the Word is still planted in my life even though the weeds have covered over everything and you cannot see it at all."

The Christian faith does not work that way. We cannot be thorny soil people and still obedient to Christ. Jesus says the weeds will choke the Word.

I think there are a lot of thorny ground people who come to church every Sunday. They are always there. They are involved in stuff. However, there is no fruit. The weeds have prevailed against the Word. Friends, I want to tell you that even if you identify yourself as a good soil person be cautious. If you saw my garden in the spring, I had my tractor out there and we plowed and laid off rows. When we finished there was nothing, there was not one weed anywhere. It was just beautiful brown soil ready to be planted.

Summer, however, end up a busy time. We had a baby and the garden was neglected. If you drove by now you would see that it is going to have to be plowed again. It is going to be a lot more work this time. We will need extra gas in the tractor. It is going to take extra time to get it done. All these weeds will have knocked down.

Friends, that is our life if we are not careful. If we are not constantly removing those weeds we will let them grow up and they will spread quickly.

The Interpretation – Good Soil People

There is a fourth group. Verse twenty says, **But those that were sown on the good soil are the ones who hear the word and accept it and bear fruit, thirtyfold and sixtyfold and a hundredfold.** These people receive the Word with joy and the harvest is great. They begin to reproduce. They begin to make more disciples. They begin to spread more seed. Is that not how planting works? Where do you get the seeds for future times, where do they come from? You say,

"We go down to the hardware store and we get more seeds." Yes, but where did they get the seed? When you plant something it grows up. It provides you with your fruit or your vegetable but what does it also provide you with? More seed. You take the seed and you plant it again. And you plant it again. And you plant it again. That is how it works.

He says here that when the Word is planted on the good soil it grows and grows and grows. It is a cycle that continues on. These people who are the good soil people hear the Word and accept the Word and then they produce a crop. They hear the Word of God as the sower is spreading it out.

With the along-the-path people it never gets started and with the rocky ground people there is just not much depth to what they know and understand. They have a very superficial fake faith. The thorny ground people get choked out. The good soil people, however, receive the Word. They accept it and produce a crop.

You may say, "Pastor, I am a Christian and that would mean that I am a good soil person." I would agree with that. I have no doubt about that. That is why, however, I would submit to you that you should understand this parable with Jesus' disciples. They understood that while they had received the Word and they were the good soil people they were also the sower. Their job was to go and to sow God's Word. Not to try to pick and choose who was going to respond. They had no idea. They would never say, "I do not think they are going to respond. I am not going to waste my seed there."

A lot of the seed got "wasted" in the process, right? For the sower a lot of it was "worthless." Maybe three-fourths of what he spread out was wasted and never did any good. It never helped anybody. Anything less that seed in the good soil is just false hope. You have these little seeds that begin to grow up and begin to do something We might look at them and say, "Look, look at what they are doing," but then they die. That is so disappointing.

We planted our garden one summer and we had tomatoes all summer. Planted more tomatoes the next summer and had a bigger garden but we harvested less stuff. That is not supposed to happen right? I mean obviously I do not have a green thumb, but that is how it is supposed to work right? You plant more tomato plants. You are supposed to get more tomatoes. Did not happen. Got less. A lot less. Did we know that going in? Certainly not! I would not have wasted my money. I would not have drove down to the plant store and bought all these tomato plants. I would not have worked outside and planted them all in the ground.

However, I did not know. When you plant, you do not know. You do not know what is going to come up. You do not know what is going to happen. You do not know if a storm is going to come. You do not know if a drought's going to come. You do not know if the animals are going to come and eat your crop. You do not know those things. You anticipate that it might happen but if you do you do not know when.

The Sower of God's Word

It is the same way as the sower of God's Word. We give it and spread it and share it and understand that it is ultimately God who is working on the hearts of these people. I do not know why some people are the beside the road people who just never got it and reject it. I do not know. I do not know why some people show this superficial faith for a little while and you think they have it. They are doing something. They are growing but then they just fall away. I do not know. If I knew the solution to that we would do something about it but I do not know. We must understand that God is the one who is changing people's hearts. Our job is to sow the seed of His Word into people's lives. I do not know if it is going to take hold. I do not know when it is going to take hold. I do not know what people are going to do with it. I only know that you and I must trust that God knows what He is doing.

I am reminded of the passage that you are very familiar with in Isaiah fifty-five. When His Word is planted, it does not return void. It accomplishes everything that He intends for it. We are sowers. We are not soil inspectors. We are not farmers that are just trying to figure it out and plan. We just need to understand this whole situation, need to act dumb. We just need to pretend like we do not know anything about farming. We have been handed this bag of seed and we have been told to just spread it. Just spread it and let God do the rest.

For me it is very discouraging sometimes. When you feel like you are out there spreading the seed and you are spreading the seed and you are sharing and you are scattering and you are planting but you do not see much happen. It is like when you walk out to that garden day after day. You wonder when are those tomatoes going to grow? You finally come to the realization one day maybe that plant's not going to happen. Or you put your fertilizer down. You watered it. You did everything you were supposed to but maybe it is just not going to happen. However, until the last

Micheal Pardue

moment when you have to stop, you keep working and planting and sowing and fertilizing and watering.

That is what we need to do. There are a bunch of people out there and in the end, it may be that they are the along the road people. There are going to be people who are rocky soil people. There are going to be people who have allowed the thorns to just rule their life. However, there is a world full of people who have good soil that when the Word is planted in their life it will grow and multiply thirty, sixty, and a hundred. For them, we just sow.

As we close, if we had a rating scale for soil, I do not where you are going to fall. Maybe it seems that you are all over the place. It might seem as if the things of this world are keeping you from following after God's Word. It might seem that you are just afraid of the difficulty that comes with being a believer in Christ. It might be that you have just flat out rejected everything that God has to offer all of your life.

Know today that if God is speaking to your heart and if He continues to speak to your heart, it may be that He wants His Word planted firmly and deeply in your life. If He continues to push you, urge you, encourage you, help you while you do not deserve it, He may be calling you to response to His Word. If He continue to expose you to His Word while you are still running, that it may be that He wants you to know the new life available in Christ.

Stop running away. Stop denying God's entrance into your life because there are four types of people here in this passage but there is only one good response to God. He desires for you to come to Him. To receive Him. To be forgiven by Him. To have new life and new hope in Him.

If you do not know Chris, the One who has told us this parable, He has exposed for you the truth of His message today. He wants His Word planted deeply inside you and He wants to guide your life. This morning if you do not know Him, let me share with you how you can know Christ. The One who came and lived a perfect life and died in our place so that we could have forgiveness. He loved us though we were people with superficial faith that allow that things of the world to come in between us and God, who had rejected God. He loved us so that we can be forgiven of that and given new life in Him.

Fellow Christ, I want you to understand you and I are sowers. See we were the good soil. God's Word firmly planted deep within us. The expectation is, however, that we would grow and that what God would do in our life would be thirty and sixty and a hundred times what was first planted in us. Now we have transitioned from being the crop that has been harvested to the one sent into the field to spread God's Word, to show others His love, and to share with them the good news of the Gospel.

Challenge

I would challenge you to understand that God has called us to sow His Word. We live in a world that is hurting and dying. We live in a world of people that need a relationship with Christ. We can plant the seed of His Word in people's lives. Maybe we do it in a direct way in directly sharing with them the good news of Christ. We must do it in the way that we live so people can see that we are different. We must share with them this good news that we have been given. I want to challenge you to think about that and pray that God would lead you to do just that.

Bibliography

Bailey, Kenneth E. *Poet & Peasant and Through Peasant Eyes: A Literary-Cultural Approach to the Parables in Luke.* Grand Rapids: William B Eerdmans Publishing Company, 1983.

Bieringer, Reimund, Florentino Gaarcía Martínez, Didier Pollefeyt, and Peter J. Tomson, . *The New Testament and Rabbinic Literature.* Leiden: Brill, 2010.

Blomberg, Craig L. *Interpreting the Parables.* Downers Grove: InterVarsity Press, 2012.

—. *Preaching the Parables* . Grand Rapids: Baker Academic , 2004.

Carlston, Charles E. *The Parables of the Triple Tradition.* Philadelphia: Fortress Press, 1975.

Caspi, Mishael, and John T. Greene. Parables and Fables As Distinctive Jewish Literary Genres: The Origins and Structure of Indirect Speech About God. Lewiston, N.Y.: Edwin Mellen Press, 2011. eBook Collection (EBSCOhost), EBSCOhost (accessed March 16, 2015).

Chilton, Bruce. *Rabbi Jesus An Intimate Biography: The Jewish LIfe and Teachings that Inspired Christianity* . New York: Doubleday, 2000.

Chilton, Bruce, and Craig Evans, . *Studying the Historical Jesus: Evaluations of the State of Current Research.* Boston: Brill, 1998.

Crossan, John Dominic. *The Power of Parable: How Fiction by Jesus Became Fiction about Jesus.* New York: HarperOne, 2012.

Drury, John. *The Parables in the Gospels* . New York: Crossroad Publishing Company, 1985.

Evans, Craig A. *Jesus and His Contemporaries: Comparative Studies.* Leiden: Brill, 1995.

Fee, Gordon D., and Douglas Stuart. *How to Read the Bible for all its Worth.* Grand Rapids: Zondervan, 2014.

Flusser, David. *The Sage from Galilee: Rediscovering Jesus' Genius.* Grand Rapids: William B Eerdmans Publishing Company, 2007 .

Halverson, Jared. M. "Of Soils and Souls: The Parable of the Sower," *The Religious Educator* 9, no. 3 (2008): 31-47, accessed March 19, 2015, https://ojs.lib.byu.edu/spc/index.php/RelEd/article/viewFile/2258/2133.

Hendrick, Charles W. *Many Things in Parables: Jesus and HIs Modern Critics.* Louisville: Westminster John Knox Press, 2004.

Huel, Donald H. "Encountering the Sower: Mark 4:1-20." *Interpretation* 56, no. 3 (July 2002): 273-283.

Hultgren, Arland J. *The Parables of Jesus: A Commentary.* Grand Rapids: William B Eerdmans Publishing Company, 2000.

Hunter, Archibald M. *Interpreting the Parables.* Philadelphia: 1960, 1960.

—. *The Parables then and Now.* Philadelphia: Westminster Press, 1971.

Jeremias, Joachim. *The Parables of Jesus .* New York: Charles Scribner's Sons, 1972.

Jones, Peter Rhea. *Studying the Parables of Jesus.* Macon: Smyth & Helwys, 1999.

—. *The Teaching of the Parables.* Nashville: Broadman Press, 1982.

Jülicher, Adolf. *Die Gleichnisreden Jesu.* Tübingen: J. C. B. Mohr, 1888.

Kennedy, Gerald. *The Parables: Sermons on the Stories Jesus Told.* New York: Harper & Brothers Publishers, 1960.

Kissinger, Warren S. *The Parables of Jesus: A History of Interpretation and Bibliography.* Lanham: Scarecrow Press, 1979.

Kistemaker, Simon J. *The Parables: Understanding the Stories Jesus Told.* Grand Rapids: Bakers Books, 1980 .

Lachs, Samuel Tobias. *A Rabbinic Commentary on the New Testament: The Gospels of Matthew, Mark and Luke.* Jersey City: KTAV Publishing, 1987.

Levison, N. *The Parables: Their Background and Local Setting.* Edinburgh: T&T Clark, 1926.

Longenecker, Richard N., ed. *The Challenge of Jesus' Parables.* Grand Rapids: William B Eerdmans Publishing Company, 2000.

Luz, Ulrich. *Matthew 8-20 Hermeneia Series.* Minneapolis: Fortress Press, 2001.

Oesterley, W. O. E. *The Gospel Parables in the Light of Their Jewish Background.* New York: The Macmillan Company , 1814.

Payne, Philip B. "The Authenticity of the Parable of the Sower and Its Interpretation," in *Gospel Perspectives*, vol. 1, ed. R.T. France and David Wenham (Sheffield: JSOT, 1980), 163-207.

Pirkei Avos: Ethics of the Fathers / A New Translation with a Commentary Anthologized from the Classical Rabbinic Sources. Brooklyn: Mesorah Publications, 2009.

Rodkinson, Michael L., trans. *The Babylonian Talmud.* Vols. 1-10. 1918.

Schweitzer, Albert. *The Quest for the Historical Jesus.* Mineola: Dover, 2005.

—. *The Quest of the Historical Jesus.* Mineola, NY: Dover Publications, 2005.

Scott, Bernard Brandon. *Hear Then the Parable: A Commentary on the Parables of Jesus.* Minneapolis: Augsburg Fortress, 1989.

Snodgrass, Klyne. *Stories with Intent: A Comprehensive Guide to the Parables of Jesus.* Grand Rapids: William B Eerdmans Publishing Company, 2008.

Stein, Robert H. *An Introduction to the Parables of Jesus.* Philadelphia : The Westminster Press, 1981.

Stern, David. *Parables in Midrash: Narrative and Exegesis in Rabbinic LIterature* . Cambridge: Harvard University Press, 1994.

Stern, Frank. *A Rabbi Looks at Jesus' Parables.* Lanham: Rowman & Littlefield Publishers, 2006.

Thoma, Clemens, and Michael Wyschogrod, . *Parable and Story in Judaism and Christianity.* Mahwah: Paulist Press, 1989.

Trench, Richard Chenevix. *Notes on the Parables of Our Lord.* New York: D. Appleton and Company, 1878.

Via, Jr., Dan Otto. *The Parables: Their Literary and Existential Dimension.* Philadelphia: Fortress, 1967.

Wenham, David. *The Parables of Jesus.* Downers Grove: IVP Academic, 1989 .

Young, Brad H. *Jesus the Jewish Theologian.* Grand Rapids: Baker Academic, 1995.

—. *Meet the Rabbis: Rabbinic Thought and the Teachings of Jesus.* Grand Rapids: Baker Academic, 2007.

—. *The Parables: Jewish Tradition and Christian Interpretation.* Grand Rapids: Baker Academic, 1998.

Zaslow, David. *Jesus: First Century Rabbi.* Brewster: Paraclete Press, 2014.

ABOUT THE AUTHOR

Micheal and his wife, Rachel, have four sons and three daughters. They make their home in Icard, NC where he is the pastor of First Baptist Church. He has severed several other churches during eleven years of vocational ministry.

He holds a B.A. in Theater Arts from Gardner-Webb University in Boiling Springs, NC, a Master of Christian Ministry from the T. Walter Brashier Graduate School at North Greenville University in Greer, SC. and a Doctor of Education from Southeastern Baptist Theological Seminary. He is also currently working on a Doctor of Philosophy at Midwestern Baptist Theological Seminary.

Micheal has had the privilege of speaking in more than fifty churches, Baptist associations, colleges, and conferences across the U.S. and internationally.

He is the author of five books, including It Shall Not Return Void from Rainer Publishing.

www.ingramcontent.com/pod-product-compliance
Lightning Source LLC
Chambersburg PA
CBHW020557030426
42337CB00013B/1128